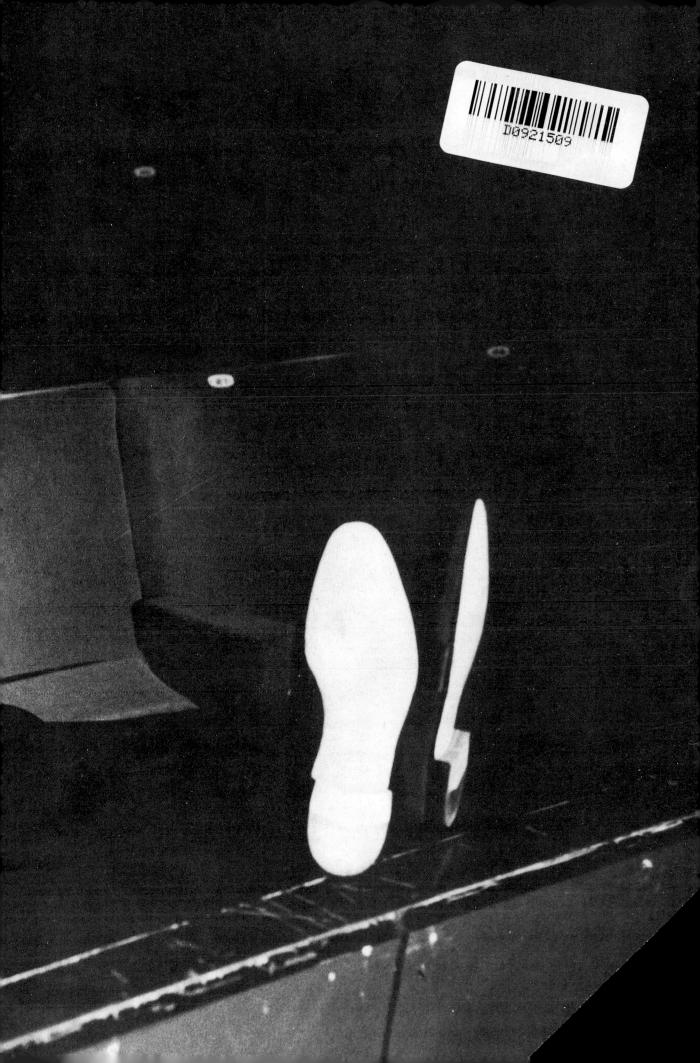

D0921509

Contents:

© 1985 GRANDREAMS LTD.

Written by John Kercher; all inside photographs supplied by and are copyright Scope Features; front cover photograph copyright Rex Features; designed by Rita Mizzi.

Published by
GRANDREAMS LIMITED,
Jadwin House, 205/211 Kentish Town Road,
London NW5 2JU.

Printed in Holland.

ISBN 0 86227 316 1

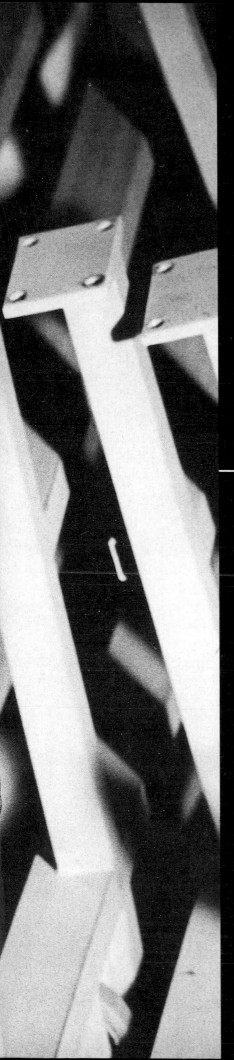

WHAM! on George's Solo Career

It seems that almost as soon as any group manages to achieve success in the charts and a good fan following everyone starts talking about the possibility of a break between the respective members.

Wham! it seems, have not escaped this either, and ever since George announced that he was going to be making a solo single, the gossip started that there was a good chance that he and Andy would go their own separate ways and establish individual careers for themselves. But both of the guys fervently deny this.

"What people don't seem to understand or appreciate," says George, "is that Andy and I aren't just a couple of guys who sing and perform together, we are friends from way back when we were kids. That bond means far more to me and Andy than anything else and we'll stick together forever.

"I think we were about twelve years old when we first met," he says. "I remember noticing Andy at school and thinking that this was the kind of guy that I'd like to know because he seemed to be interesting and I could talk to him more easily than most people. Also we had a lot of interests in common. The fact that we've not fallen out with each other so far should prove to most people that we can stick together through

WHAM! on George's Solo Career

thick and thin. And when you've struggled for some kind of success as we have then you can appreciate friendship a lot more."

Even so, when George stepped into the recording studio and his solo effort of the song *'Careless Whisper'*, it looked almost certain that it might just tempt him towards thinking of doing more on his own. The single rocketed up the charts to the top position where it stayed for some weeks, selling more than a million copies in Britain alone, which was more than the success of any previous *Wham!* record.

So why was it that he decided to do it by himself and not put it out on the *Wham!* name?

"It was essential that it had to be a solo effort because there wasn't the choice to make it a *Wham!* style record," says George. "We wrote the song between us, so it wasn't entirely all my own work, and the song was, in fact, written some time ago before we'd even managed to sign a recording deal. It was written around the same time as *'Young Guns'* and so on, but because we were launching ourselves as a duo at the time, it was inopportune to try and establish the song as a solo effort.

"But between putting out the *Wham!* products we felt that it would be nice to give this one a try, and so I just went in and did it. I

WHAM! on George's Solo Career

was quite surprised with the enormous success and popularity that it enjoyed."

However, did George's solo achievement make Andy feel an 'outsider' in any way?

"Not at all. You've got to remember that I did co-write the song, and so there was my stamp on it even if I didn't sing on the record. I see it as just another *Wham!* project. It was obvious that if we were going to put it out at all, then it would have to be George who sang it, because it was much better suited to his kind of voice than mine.

"In fact, I wouldn't say that I had a good singing voice at all. I'm fine when I'm harmonizing, but I don't think I have quite the strength or power in my voice that he has. I must admit that I do envy him his singing talents. I'm not jealous of them, because that's to put a whole different interpretation on things. But I do often wish that I could sing as well as him."

On this basis, Andy is quite emphatic that he won't be doing any solo recordings. But as for George, is there a chance that he might continue with more efforts by himself.

"I've often fancied the idea of doing an album which is completely made up of cover versions of other people's songs," he says. "Most groups or singers write their own material nowadays, and you don't get that situation you had in the 1950s or 1960s where

WHAM! on George's Solo Career

someone would produce a song and any number of people would record it.

"There are some really good songs around that I'd like to be able to put a new interpretation to. I think that people like to hear variations on songs they like. But the project is going to take some thinking about because I would want to make absolutely certain that each piece of material was perfect!"

Andy also thinks that this would be a good idea. "The thing about George is," he says, "that he can write some beautiful songs. But he often tends to just write the song, rather than thinking of himself as being the person who is going to have to do it on record. This often means that whilst he comes up with a great song, the way it is structured isn't ideally suited to the kind of voice that he has.

"Maybe someday he'll do some for other artists because it's a shame to waste good material. It's really a case of trying to understand your own voice and just what you can do with it, and then write songs that match it perfectly. I'm sure that he'll be able to do this and then you'll really hear some great songs.

"But meanwhile, if he wants to do any more solo stuff then the idea of cover versions is a good one."

George's solo success did, however, produce a new attitude in the way that the press saw *Wham!* Whereas before,

WHAM! on George's Solo Career

people had been clamouring for interviews with both of the guys, suddenly it became a situation where it was George who was getting all of the attention. Whenever the 'phone rang in the *Wham!* press office, the request for an interview was always with George because *'Careless Whisper'* had suddenly become such a monster hit.

It would have been easy for George to have revelled in his new found solo fame and just gone ahead and made the most of it. But what the fans don't know is that he is not that kind of person. He thinks too much of Andy as a friend to just shut him out like that. So he made certain he would only do so many interviews and the rest should be done with Andy. He didn't want him sitting around when, essentially, he had been co-writer of the song.

Also, even before the success of the record, when George had flown to Florida to film the video that was to promote the single, he took Andy along with him. It should be quite apparent from actions like this that any rumours about *Wham!* splitting for separate recording careers is out of the question.

"There's no need for it anyway," says Andy. "In any group people should feel free to do things that are outside of the band whilst still being a part of that group for other projects. We're together for good!"

The WHAM! Story

The town of Bushey in Hertfordshire had no idea that 1963 was going to be a landmark in its history. Not exactly known for its output of pop musicians, the birth of Andrew John Ridgeley on the 26th January of that year and of George Michael on the 25th June, was just another event.

But little did the people of that town realise that they'd be firmly on the map by the early 1980s when these couple of young guys would burst onto the music scene and become international stars, topping the charts in America as well as being regular faces in all of the newspapers and magazines.

The town has become important for George and Andy, despite the fact that they often moaned about the lack of activity there when they were at school.

"But we weren't too much into going and watching 'live' groups perform," says George, "so it didn't bother us too much." Andy says that he felt quite at home in the quiet suburban atmosphere and gets a great thrill even now from being able to take a walk around some of his old haunts as a kid.

"I know that one of the places I always went to was the park. It was a kind of central meeting area for me and all of my friends, and all the girls would go there too. I'd play football there as well at every opportunity that I could," he says. "It's funny to walk around there now and enjoy those memories. I liked the people in the town too, because they weren't and still aren't, pretentious at all. In a way, I'm pleased that I grew up here and not in a huge city."

It was a love of music and records that brought Andrew and George together at school. "I liked to go to Watford to buy records on a Saturday morning," says Andy. "There weren't many shops in Bushey where I could do that."

George remembers meeting Andy when they'd just started at senior school. "I saw him and the way that he was talking about things and I felt that here was someone I wanted to know and be friends with. From the moment we met we really hit it off and all we seemed to talk about was music."

The guys would often go around to each other's houses playing records and when they got older, used to occasionally, when they could afford it, go dancing at the discos in Watford. "We did have quite a few friends and it became a sort of weekly get together to go to the dances. That's about the time we became friends with Shirley too. She was always with us. She was a good dancer too!" It was she who would later form an integral part of Wham!'s debut single.

Whilst George stayed on at school to complete his studies, Andy left to go to College to further his education, although the guys were still seeing each other regularly and discussing musical ideas and socialising. The real test of their strength came when they both found themselves on the dole. George had a job for a while and during the daytime Andy would be working on ideas for songs. They'd now decided that they'd like to try for a career in music if only they could come up with the right commercial sound.

"The only thing we really had to go on was the records we'd been collecting for years," says George. "In a way, we were quite untainted by any performing bands because we didn't go to watch many. The fact that we were later on the dole for quite a time meant that we didn't have the necessary cash to be able to finance any expensive equipment for ourselves either in the way of instruments

or recording gear."

Andy had become proficient on guitar to the extent that they could use it as some back-up, and they also had the use of a drum box, which helped tremendously. It seems strange that they were working in complete isolation from most musical influences which other groups have been subjected to. "We were also fortunate in having a few friends who had some better recording gear than us and we occasionally went there or borrowed it.

"Most of the day was spent writing and trying to rehearse our own compositions. We knew that if we were to stand any chance of landing a recording contract with one of the major companies then it would have to be on demos of our own compositions and not cover versions. You need to be able to show them that you are capable of sustaining some kind of creative output."

From this period, the guys managed to put together, 'Wham Rap', 'Bad Boys' and 'Careless Whisper'. But it was 'Young Guns, Go For It' that was to eventually put them on the map. And they did it in style. "When we began working on it and putting the whole thing down on tape," says George, "we

could see from the way that it was working out, that it was much more than just a straightforward song. The lyrics and the entire structure of the thing presented its way to us more in the format of a small playlet.

"There was a kind of conversation that was going on and so Andy, Shirley and I put it across that way and did the video that accompanied it in the same way." It certainly added much more drama and was a contributing factor to the success of their single. But they were also accused at the time of its release of trying to imitate the rapping style that was current, which they fervently deny!

Andy says: "For a start, we didn't sit down and consciously write the song the way that it was. It just came out that way. The rapping style wasn't 'current' then, as a lot of people seem to think. It had been going in America for ages and, if anything, had run its course there.

"Besides, to try and cash in on a craze is a bit ridiculous because no matter how much you plan something to coincide with a fashion, you've probably missed the boat by the time the record is released. So we never tried to manipulate the market in that sense.

The only way that you can hope for success is to just write what you want to write and then hope that everyone else likes it too.'' In Wham!'s case they did, and they had found a recipe for good commercial songs which has managed to provide them with a consistent output of hit material.

What was attractive about the original Wham! releases was the excellent choreography they used, which George and Andy say was the result of their love of dancing.

''Shirley always danced with us at the discos and we decided to elaborate on the original kind of routines that we used in the clubs. When we went to the local club, it was always the thing to try and develop your own style so that you'd be a bit different from everyone else. So when we came to doing the videos we thought we'd use that.''

Wham! had not, as yet, faced a real live audience on tour. For a start, they needed much more material in order to be able to do that, but they did try to attempt to break into the American market. They went over to do some promotional gigs on television and the reaction was a good one. Their debut on US television was for the show 'American

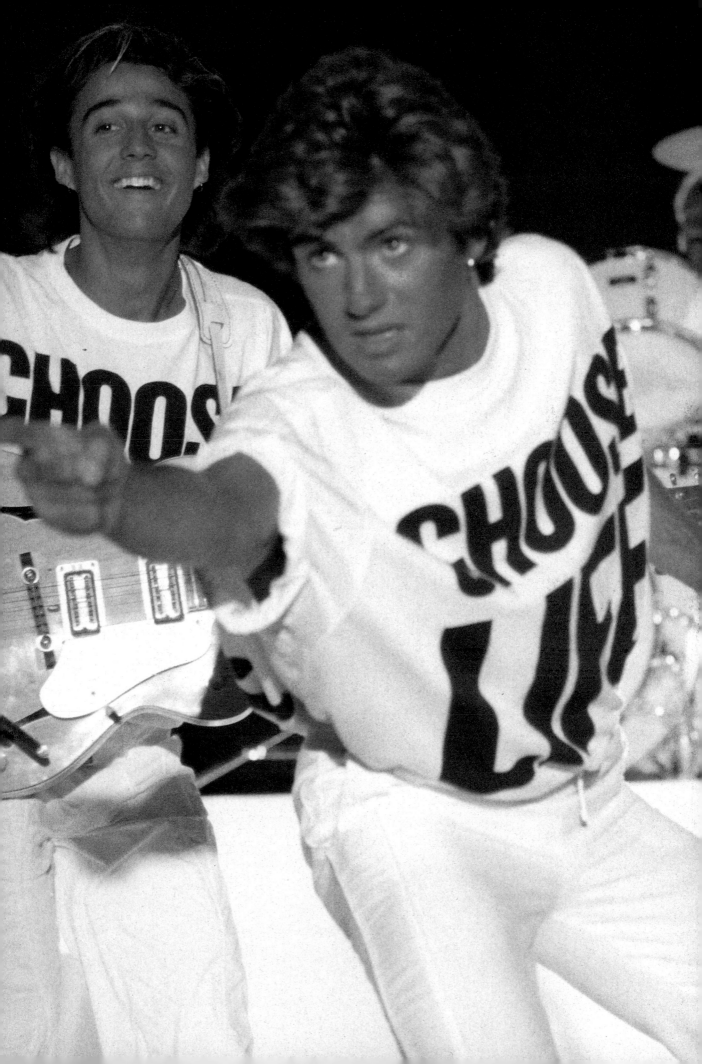

Bandstand' *which has the kind of long running record that* 'Top Of The Pops' *has in Britain.*

It was not without event. Just as with most television shows of this kind, the audience is enticed to make a fair noise and show enthusiasm for each of the acts that perform. But in the case of Wham!, *the audience was genuinely impressed and when the guys completed their set, the cheering continued.*

Despite what seemed like a good reception on television it did not transfer itself quite so dramatically in terms of record sales. In order to really crack the American market, most bands find that they have to tour for quite a while in order to establish themselves in every state. It was also difficult for new bands from both Britain and America to make themselves heard because of the policy of radio stations to concentrate on middle of the road groups. It was MTV, the 24 hour music station, which pushed out videos non stop and by request to assess their popularity which helped many groups break through. Wham! returned to Britain in an attempt to put their first tour together, with the smash hit album, 'Fantastic', *behind them.*

"We wanted to put together a show that the fans would really remember," says George. "We didn't want to just go out on stage and leap about to the music, but put together a good piece of theatre too. It was all carefully organized, the music, the choreography, the costumes and when we felt we were ready we went out and did it!"

The tour was an enormous success with Shirley, and Wham!'s other girl performer, D.C. Lee contributing much to the vocal and visual elements of the programme. D.C. Lee has since gone on to her own solo career, and was replaced by another girl, Pepsi at the time.

However, in the middle of the tour, George went on stage and found that he had lost his voice! It was the moment that every singer dreads and George was ordered to rest his voice for several weeks before continuing with the tour.

That Wham! *did.* They had tried a novel way of putting their concerts to the fans, dividing the show into two halves with the middle section showing a series of home movies of the guys as kids. "It was a lot of fun and we think the fans had a good laugh watching us on holiday

27

or messing around when we were much younger."

Wherever the guys played, the theatres were packed to capacity, and the stage was flooded with

presents of soft toys. From this tour, Wham! went on to Japan before returning to Britain and going back into the studio.

Since then they have continued to turn

out the hits, and despite people assuming that they would fade they have gone on to make an even greater impression than even they would have

thought possible. With George's solo, 'Careless Whisper' going into the million sales, and 'Freedom' following it, not to mention, the album 'Make It Big' also going platinum in the number one position, Wham! have also topped the American chart with 'Wake Me Up Before You Go Go', making 1984 a year to remember in their history! Now it looks like an American tour is the next thing, along with the Far East and Australia and the future looks as bright as the smiles on both Andy's and George's faces.

WHAM!
~ The Pressures of Success

It was no freak coincidence that the first major Wham! tour was sponsored by a sportswear company. The guys were regularly seen on stage wearing sparkling white T-shirts and shorts. "I think it suited our image perfectly," says Andy. That's quite true because he is a bit of a fanatic when it comes to keeping fit and is also keen on competitive sports.

"Ever since I was a kid I was interested in winning at something. That's probably why at school I was always playing football. I played for the school team and was forever watching matches. In fact I even contemplated the idea of trying to become a professional footballer at one time, but the competition to get in to a proper team is so great that I gave up on the idea. You can spend years training and still not make the first eleven. So I now satisfy my football mania by being a spectator.

"Manchester United are the team that I've faithfully supported for as long as I can remember. I'd go and see them whenever they're playing if I could, but it's not so easy to do now and I have to make do with watching them on 'Match Of The Day'. Both George and I sit down and watch that every week if we can!"

Andy's other interests extend to the snowy slopes in Austria and Italy where he has also acquired an interest in skiing!

"I'm not all that good at it," he laughs. "After watching the top class stars doing it on television I thought that I'd be able to do that some day, but being realistic I know that it's not possible. But I first became interested in the sport when I went on a school trip to Austria. I promised myself that some day I'd go back there and have a go at it.

"I did too. And I enjoyed it, and I started taking holidays in the winter just so that I could go to the ski resorts. I'll probably keep on going for the fun of it."

Holidays are a major

31

WHAM!
~ The Pressures of Success

occupation for Wham! who seem to find any excuse that they can to get away and replenish their sun tan. "Why not?" says George. "We work really hard for most of the year and instead of allocating a couple of weeks to a total holiday, we try and fit them in all the time and make it combined pleasure and business trips.

"That was one of the reasons that we went to do the 'Make It Big' album abroad. It does help taxwise, but I think we'd have done it anyway. It was lovely to be able to sun ourselves in the South of France in between doing recording work in the studio."

Andy, on the other hand is insistent about just how they spend their time. "You won't find us wasting our time sunning ourselves on a beach and doing absolutely nothing. That would be far too boring. We like to involve ourselves in strenuous activities when we're on holiday. Things like volleyball and swimming which keep us fit as well as providing us with some fun.

"We aren't too hot on the idea of going on holiday alone either. There are some people who like the idea of being a recluse for a few weeks, but that's not us at all. If I had my way, I'd go on holiday with a crowd of friends. I think you can have much more fun when there are a lot of you together.

"So after the beach we go in search of good clubs to do some dancing and things like that. A holiday for us is a way of totally getting rid of any tension. And if we're combining it with work in the studio, then it tunes our mind up and keeps us mentally alert too. I don't think we'd be able to work so hard if

WHAM!
~The Pressures of Success

we lazed around in between. We have to keep the adrenaline flowing in some way or another."

So far, Wham! are making their way holidaywise slowly around the world, stopping off at places that interest them. And you can't get much more exotic than Hawaii, despite the fact that it is Americanized.

"That happened on the offchance," says George. "We had to go to Japan to do some promotional work. It was quite a unique experience being in Tokyo because it is so technological there and yet still quite traditional too. But we'd bought a 'plane ticket that allowed us to travel almost around the world on it. So whilst we were in Japan we just said, 'why don't we go to Hawaii'. It seemed like a good idea and we'd always wanted to travel there, so that's what we did.

We had a terrific time."

Andy reckons that it was school that started him on his holiday mania. "We were always going on trips here, there and everywhere and not always abroad. I remember that there was one where we went to Wales and another down in Dorset. But of course, the teachers were always with us. The first time I ever went away without any teachers and parents was quite an experience!"

Wham! also like to be mobile when they go away. "We'll always hire a car or a bike or whatever transport's available to us. It means that we don't need to be stuck in the town for the duration of our stay but can get out and see something of the place. I remember that we went to Greece, to the island of Corfu, and there was this place renting out mopeds. Well, I hired

one and within a few minutes of getting on it, I crashed. I felt so embarrassed about having to take the thing back!''

When you are so busy as the guys from Wham! are you find that it's not just a case of trying to relax, but also keeping in good shape for the tours.

"It's absolutely essential to be physically fit," says George. "Because there's really no way that you can sustain yourself on a tour if you don't keep your body well tuned. We use a lot of energy on stage and give a good 100%. ■

if we didn't keep fit with some kind of work-outs or sports then we'd be in the position of cancelling dates, which is something we'd never like to do.

"Really you have to gear yourself like an Olympic athlete in training. It might sound a bit like an exaggeration, but it's quite true. There are quite a few groups who've discovered just how demanding a tour can be!"

But this doesn't mean that all of their activities are energetic! Andy, for instance, is a motor racing fan. "It's just one of those sports that I

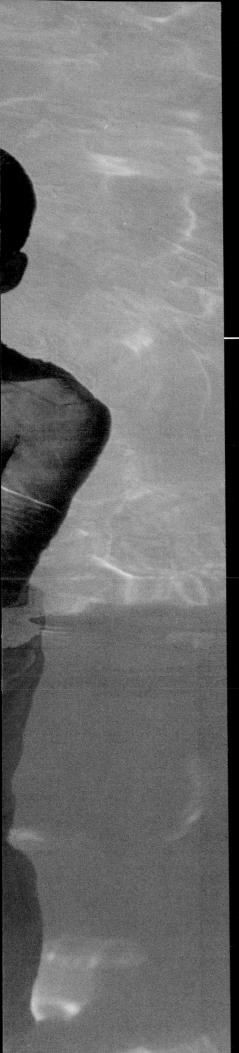

WHAM!
~ The Pressures of Success

find really exciting. I try to watch all of the major races on television and I even thought about the possibility of going in a race myself some day. But the costs of the sport are tremendous and so I don't think it'll be a reality. But I might have a go at a rally some day. They can be just as exciting!"

Another way in which he might fulfil his driving ambition is to go to America for a really long holiday!

"What really appeals to me," he says, "is the idea of flying there and then hiring a car so that we could drive right across and around the entire country. When we travel there for touring or promotional work we only see a few of the cities. It'd be nice to be able to take our time and tour at our leisure around the South, the Grand Canyon, and see all of those marvellous places that we've only

watched on television. Maybe we might even try to go as far as Mexico.

"The only problem for us is fitting in such a project, but it's definitely something I'm planning to do some time."

The guys also believe in travelling with the minimum of luggage when they go abroad. "We hate the idea of all the hassles at airports with too many suitcases and things. If we had our way, we'd just fly out with no more than a book and buy all our clothes when we got there.

"Holidays should be as easy and relaxing as possible as far as we're concerned. And there's enough problems at customs as there is. We're not really the kind of people who spend days wandering around souvenir shops when we're away. We're too preoccupied with enjoying

39

WHAM!
~The Pressures of Success

ourselves. We do take
quite a few
photographs or home
movies though,
because they provide

When they aren't
living it up in some
exotic place then you
can often find Andy
and George with an old

WHAM!
and their music

If anyone was of the opinion that *Wham!* were going to be one hit wonders, then their list of chart successes has certainly disproved it. Like any group starting out, Andy and George used to sit at home and wait for the new listing to come out every week to see just where their new release had risen to. But now that they seem to have consolidated their position as one of Britain's most consistent selling groups, they have become a bit more relaxed in their attitude to their records.

"I think," says Andy, "that after a while you begin to realise that it is the consistency of the popularity of the group or the songs that is more important than anything else. Just because a new record of ours doesn't reach the number one position doesn't mean that it is any worse a song than the one before. The charts work in a strange way. It is quite possible to be in the top five of the charts and sell more than the record that occupies the number one position. It's the durability of the record in the charts that counts.

"There was a time when I'd really be looking to see if we were at number one, but it doesn't bother me any more," he says.

"We've become firmly established now and, even though I say it myself, I do feel that we're one of the best bands in the country now."

However, he does admit that he feels that any new *Wham!* record ought to automatically go into the charts. "It's not a case of being blasé about it, but I think that the record buyers now know that a single of ours should be a good one and that we won't let them down. But as long as it's up in the top of the charts somewhere, then I'm quite content."

He says that too much stress is probably placed on the Top Twenty. "People don't seem to regard the album charts in the same way that they do singles charts," he says. "If an album sits comfortable half way up for months on end, nobody worries, and it could well produce a high selling figure. That's the way that I like to look at things."

Luckily for *Wham!* they can take that attitude because all of their albums so far have gone straight in at the top and made them one of the best selling artists for some time. George and Andy are also realistic about the other good bands around which present a record rivalry to them.

"Not everyone can be at the top," says George. "When you've got groups like *Frankie Goes To Hollywood*, *Duran Duran*, *Culture Club*, *Spandau Ballet* and any number of other good acts around, and all releasing records around the same time, then it's bound to be a bit like a game of chess in the charts. People are shuffling about all the time. It doesn't mean that anyone is better than anyone else."

Just how *Wham!* keep on coming up with the hits is the envy of many a band, but George and Andy seem to manage it, even if, as Andy explains, the circumstances which produce their creativity are odd, to say the least, at some times.

"The single that we put out just before Christmas in 1984 was an example of how ideas for songs can suddenly come to you," laughs George. "You think of someone sitting down at a piano or with a guitar and tape machine and really working hard at it. In this instance, Andy and I were sitting together at my house and we were watching *'Match Of The Day'* in the evening. We'd just been chatting and cheering on the teams, when suddenly I yelled out and ran upstairs."

Andy was equally

surprised. "I wondered what on earth he was up to," he laughs. "He seemed to be up there ages and I went to see what was going on. When I found him, he was singing into his tape recorder and when he'd finished he just turned and told me that he'd had a marvellous song come into his head whilst he'd been watching television and that if he hadn't rushed upstairs to put the ideas down then he'd probably have forgotten it."

So you can now appreciate why songwriters despair when they're on a bus or in a taxi and don't have the means to put their ideas down, other than the back of an envelope. And you can't put many lyrics onto a bus ticket! It's why so many group members now seem to take either a tape machine with them or one of those miniature keyboards that has a memory in it!

So far, the early days of *Wham!*, when they were struggling on the dole and making music in their own homes, have provided them with all of their hit records, although new material has naturally been written for the albums.

Just how many more potential hit records are sitting at home waiting to be recorded? "We've now completely exhausted all of that early material," says George. "We only worked carefully on a few songs which we felt would help us get a recording deal. A few we held back and did later, but *'Careless Whisper'* was really the last of that early output. It's now down to the tough work of producing a steady stream of new material, and it isn't easy. But we both love the whole process of writing songs. It's exciting to come up with an idea and then go into the studio and watch the whole thing come together.

"When people then go out and buy that song in their hundreds of thousands it's a rewarding experience!"

What Andy and George
think of each other

It is because Andy and George are such good friends, that they find it quite easy to be able to have a go at each other, either privately or in public in a humorous way without hurting each other's feelings too much, although they don't exactly mince words and can be quite cutting when they want to be.

This, however, is often tempered with the fact that they can have sly digs at themselves too. Talking about George, the mischievous Andy says: "If there's really one thing about George that annoys me no end, it's his total devotion to his hairstyle. It drives me absolutely crazy the way he spends so much time on it, making certain that it's perfect before we meet any of the public.

"As for me, I can do a quick comb job and I'm ready to go. But he'll be standing there in front of the mirror making sure everything's in place and just when I think he's finished, back he'll go again for another quick comb! I'm always onto him about that, but it doesn't seem to make any difference.

The criticism just runs off him like water off a duck's back."

That said, Andy admits that from the moment he met George he liked him. "There was just something about him that made me think, 'I want to know this guy. He'd be a good friend!' And that's just the way that things have turned out I'm pleased to say."

Both of the guys love the occasional party, although Andy says: "George is probably much more of an extrovert than I am."

George, on the other hand, feels that Andy can be just as much a show-off when he wants to be. "You want to see him when he's had too much to drink," he laughs. "Many's the time I've had to be the shoulder to support him on the way home." Andy just laughs at this.

"I think George is maybe more of the ladies' man. I'm sure he loves all that female attention. But then what fella wouldn't. Myself, I tend to like to have a steady girlfriend than a different one every night or week. I can't see the point of that. I'd much rather have the opportunity of developing a good relationship and really getting to understand someone."

George has his own feelings on Andy. "He tends to let the cat slip out of the bag more than I would," he says. "Many is the time that we've decided to keep something quiet so that we can have a bit of peace and relaxation and he's gone and blurted it out at the first opportunity. Like there was this time we were going abroad and we didn't really want too many people to know because we had a chance to take a week's holiday. So what does Andy do? He has to appear on this television show one morning and during the course of the interview he's asked what we're going to be doing and he tells millions of people exactly where and when we are going. Off we fly, and the next thing that we know is that we're completely surrounded by fans and all of their families wanting to chat and get autographs. And this is abroad. All of those fans who were going to the same place knew exactly where we were. And when I wondered how they could possibly have found out, Andy looks at me all innocently and admits that he mentioned it casually on television!"

People had a field day when Andy was reported to have gone into hospital to have his nose altered. The stories of the day seemed to imply that he had been at a night club making merry and that his other friend, David Austin, had haphazardly swung an ice bucket in the air and the unfortunate Andy had happened to get in the way. The result of this supposed incident was that Andy had a gash and somewhat bent nose to thank for it.

But Andy has since denied that this was true and that the whole thing was a fabrication.

"It wasn't true either that I went to have the operation on my nose, just because I was vein. It wasn't done for cosmetic reasons at

all," he says.

"When I was a kid I had problems with the inner part of my nose, and I was told that it would be possible to have it all corrected when I was twenty one years old. Well, as soon as I reached that age in 1983 I made the arrangement to go and have it attended to. That was the real reason. But it didn't turn out as well as I wanted it to. The lining of my nose didn't set the way it should have done and they don't seem to be able to do anything about it. So I'm stuck with it now!"

Do either of the guys find the other almost unbearable to be with at times? "No, I don't think so," says George, "because we know just how to keep each other in line. We know what we're really like. In fact we're quite different privately from the way we present ourselves on stage.

"You've got to be honest about the job of being a pop star. A lot of them aren't. They believe that they are the people they are on stage in real life. That's not being realistic. I'd much rather let people know that being a pop musician, singer or

whatever is like being in show business. It's a show you're putting on and when you go on stage you have to be larger than life. You need to strut and be a bit cocky up there, leading the audience on and making out you're the star. It's what they expect. But when you come off that stage, you become yourself. It's the same with our music. It's pop music. We're not ashamed of that. If we wanted to be a cult band we'd have gone about things quite differently."

That said, George does remember a time when he felt Andy was getting to be a bit too much.

"It was just after he left school. He left a bit before me and so there he was all worldly and knowing. It didn't damage our friendship but he was a bit hard to live with for a while." Andy laughs at that. He doesn't agree with it and mentions that he could probably think up something quite similar of George if he wanted to.

"I think he's changed a bit since we met, but then everyone does, don't they."

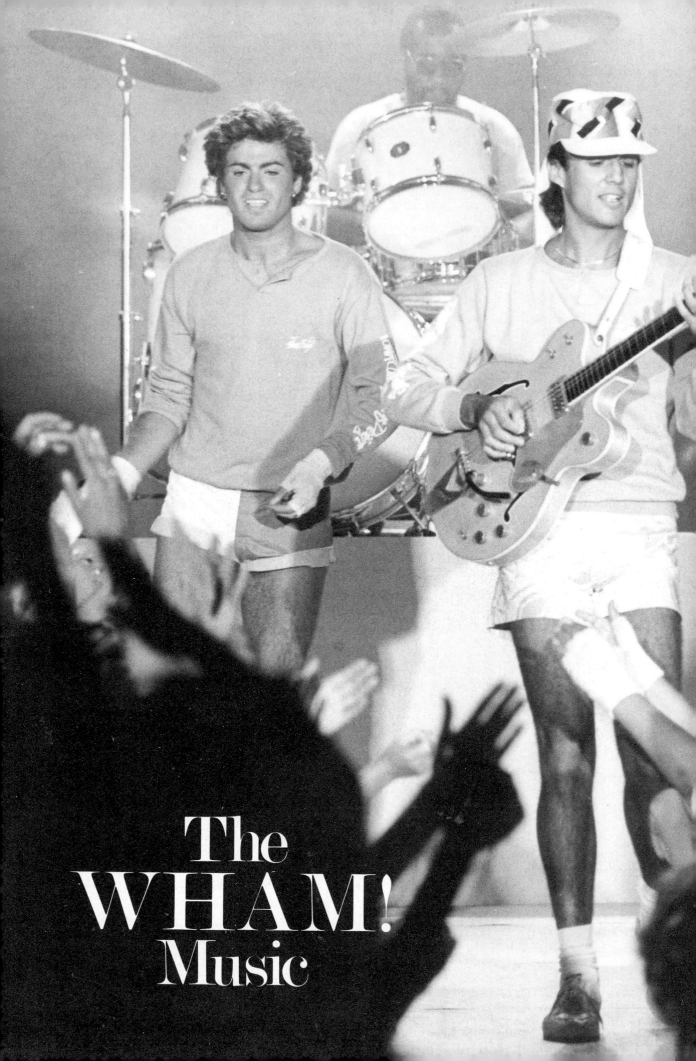

The
WHAM!
Music

The reason that Wham! are as successful as they are is not just down to the deep sun tans, George's hunky figure, the sexy eyes and good looks. The real answer is in their highly commercial songs which seem to be carrying the duo forwards to some kind of record for number one hits. Most groups would be pleased with one a year of the calibre Wham! turn out, but these guys notched up three in 1984 alone which is not bad when you think that they are prepared to take risks in the material that they put out.

You would be hard pushed to find such a contrast in styles between say, 'Young Guns', 'Freedom' and their 1984 Christmas single, 'Last Christmas' which was very traditional. All things considered, their records are good to dance to, and that's what half of the market is about these days. You can have the most beautiful looks in the world, but fans are fickle when it comes to pin-ups, and you aren't going to keep on selling records in their millions if you base your success solely on looks alone. That said, it certainly hasn't done George and Andy any harm!

So just how difficult is it for them to write songs that sell in the quantities they do?

"The problem we and most groups have to face is that the first album is always the easiest," says Andy. "You've been struggling for a while to get some material together and you tend to build up quite a few songs which you hope to make some demos of. In our case, we weren't in the position of having dozens of songs to choose from. We only did a few which we really worked at to try and get perfection. With the first album, at least we had some stuff we could use, but as the next couple came along things obviously got tougher.

"We aren't able to go back home now and look through a pile of tapes for something we can work on. There

isn't anything, so it all has to be fresh and George and I either work independently or together to try and come up with new ideas. I think that what is interesting, from our point, is that whilst we are naturally looking for something which is commercial in approach and sound, we aren't limiting ourselves to a specific type of song.

"We feel quite happy to experiment with anything so long as it's a good song with a strong and meaningful lyric. Nowadays, we don't go straight into the studio with everything worked out note perfect and just lay the tracks down. We tend to establish some kind of framework for the songs and then go into the studio and take it from there, building as we go along."

What some bands do is to overwrite material for an album by often as much as half a dozen songs, that then provides them with the opportunity to select the best. "But we don't do that," laughs Andy. "It's tough enough writing just enough for the album. Maybe we'll do a couple of extra songs just in case what we've got doesn't match up with what we want. But that's it. Just enough as is necessary. Songwriting is a tough

business. Especially when people are constantly comparing what you've done with your last album.''

Wham! *have so far produced three albums in their career since they appeared on the music scene in November 1982 with the single 'Young Guns'. The first was the incredibly successful, 'Fantastic' which rushed straight to the number one position in the album charts following on the success of their debut hit.*

With the single, 'Bad Boys' giving them an equal success, they launched their second album, 'Club Tropicana' in the summer of 1983. ''A lot of people thought that doing that cover with its sun tan appeal was overdoing things a bit,'' *says Andy.* ''But we love holidays and this was a nice way of doing things.''

'Wake Me Up Before You Go Go', came out in the Spring of 1984 and was followed by George's solo effort, the phenomenal, million selling, 'Careless Whisper', which only just led the Wham! single, 'Freedom'. It must have been one of the quickest double products in the singles charts, both reaching number one position, for a long while.

But just how do

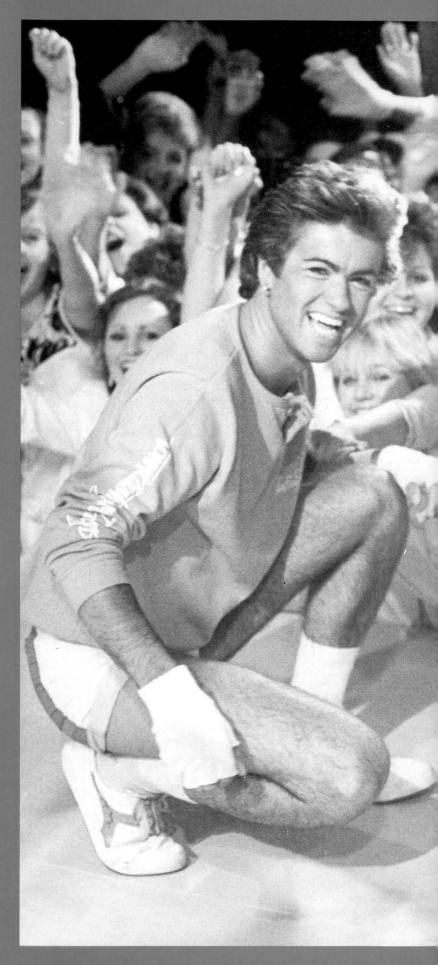

Andy and George cope with promoting their singles and do they still find the recording process exciting?

"I think that for me," says Andy, "the real high comes from the early stages of recording. I like that a lot because it's the first time that we really get to hear what songs are going to sound like on record. Also, we're still putting the material together in a sense. I really enjoy the producing aspects of the business. But I don't really like the whole promotional thing. I know that it's essential to get records sold, but it can become boring after a while.

"I suppose it's like anything. That once you've completed the job, you want to get on with the next thing. But then in any creative thing like this you've got to follow up with the selling of the thing or you've wasted all that time.

"Probably what gets to me most is when we have lots of televison programmes. I can't adapt all that easy to the chat shows. They seem a bit unnatural. And whilst I don't mind the pop magazine side of things, I do tend to dislike some of the heavier music papers because they can become a bit negative or pretentious."